MW01254526

**A Bite-Sized Brexit Book**

# Economic Growth Post Brexit

## How the UK Should Take on the World

## John Mills

Cover design by Dean Stockton
Published by Bite-Sized Books Ltd 2019
©John Mills 2019

ISBN: 9781097402427

Bite-Sized Books Ltd Cleeve Road, Goring RG8 9BJ UK
information@bite-sizedbooks.com
**Registered in the UK. Company Registration No: 9395379**

# Contents

About the Author      2

**John Mills**

Introduction      3

**This book has an uplifting message**

Chapter 1      5

**Imbalances**

Chapter 2      26

**Solutions**

Chapter 3      44

**Conclusion**

Bite-Sized Public Affairs Books      46

Bite-Sized Books Catalogue      48

# About the Author

## John Mills

John Mills is an entrepreneur and economist who has long been involved with political affairs. He is the founder and chairman of John Mills Limited (JML), which specialises in selling high volume consumer products, using audio-visual methods for promoting their sale both in the UK and in many other countries – about 85 at the last count. His main interests as an economist are the UK's relationship with the EU and the relatively poor performance of the western economies compared with those in the East.

He was for many years a senior Labour elected member of Camden Council, the London Boroughs Association and the Association of Metropolitan Authorities, and in the late 1980s he was deputy chairman of the London Dockland Development Corporation. He was chairman and then deputy chairman of Vote Leave, joint chairman of Business for Britain and the founder of Labour Leave, all campaigning for Brexit during the run-up to the June 2016 EU referendum. He is on the board of open Democracy, vice-chairman of the Economic Research Council and founder of both The Pound Campaign and Labour Future, all concerned in different ways with the UK's economic and political prospects, He is a frequent commentator on TV and radio and he has a large number of published books, articles, pamphlets and blogs to his credit.

## Introduction

# This book has an uplifting message

This book has an uplifting message. It is that we could get our economy to grow much faster and more sustainably than it has done recently. Over the last dozen years our growth rate has been 1.4% per annum, which is 60% below the 3.5% world average.[1] We could do very much better than this because our poor performance has not been caused by inevitable forces. It is the result of policy mistakes which could – and should – have been avoided.

During the first 25 years after the war, the average growth rate among western economies was close to 4%. Between 1975 and 2000, this dropped to about 3%. Since 2000 it has been barely 1.5%.[2] The UK is not, therefore unique in seeing its performance decline, but it is a relatively extreme case.

Growth at this rate is not sufficient to avoid real wages for most people in the UK stagnating or falling. It undermines faith and confidence in our government ruling elite. It generates widening inequalities between the regions of the country, between the generations and between those whose wealth is steadily increasing and those who have no such luck. It leaves the UK as a nation steadily falling further and further behind other countries, losing more and more status and influence in the world.

We very badly need to get our growth rate up to somewhere close to the world average. This book explains how this could be done, explores the risks in adopting the radical changes in policy which would be required, but balances these against the probably very heavy downside consequences of continuing as we are.

1. Data in successive issues of *International Financial Statistics Yearbook*. Washington DC: IMF various dates.
2. Ibid

# Chapter 1

# Imbalances

The UK economy is growing so slowly because it is extraordinarily unbalanced. We invest far less of our GDP than most other countries do, and the investments we do make are largely not in the most productive areas.

We have deindustrialised to a dangerous – arguably reckless – extent. Our very large balance of payments deficits year after year highlight our inability to pay our way in the world. These deficits also reflect the fact that we enjoy a standard of living which is considerably higher than we are actually earning.

To finance it we have - every year - to sell national assets and to borrow more and more money, increasingly losing control over our economy in the process. Inequalities – both regional, inter-generational and socio-economic - are becoming so wide that they are in danger of tearing our social fabric apart.

## Investment

In the UK, we devote barely 16% of our national income every year to investment in our future. This figure includes intellectual property, such as computer software. Excluding intellectual property, physical investment has recently been running at around 12% of GDP[1] – more or less equal to the depreciation charge on existing assets, so that there is no net increase every year.[2]

The world average for total investment as a percentage of GDP is over 50% higher than ours, at 26%. In China, the figure has recently hovered round 45%.[3]

## Table 1.1

### GROSS INVESTMENT, SOCIAL RATES OF RETURN AND GROWTH RATES - FOR SELECTED COUNTRIES AND PERIODS

| Country | | Period | Gross Investment % of GDP | Average Social Rate of Return | Average Growth Rate |
|---------|---|--------|---------------------------|-------------------------------|---------------------|
| UK | | 1934-1941 | 14% | 37% | 5.6% |
| USA | | 1939-1944 | *7%* | *144%* | *10.1%* |
| Japan | | 1953-1970 | 29% | 35% | 10.1% |
| China | | 2002-2012 | 37% | 25% | 9.1% |
| Korea | | 2005-2016 | 30% | 12% | 3.5% |
| Singapore | | 2005-2016 | 26% | 20% | 5.3% |
| UK | | 2005-2016 | 17% | 8% | 1.4% |
| World | | 2005-2016 | 26% | 14% | 3.5% |

Source: The Social Rate of Return is calculated as the ratio between total investment and total increase in GDP over a long enough period -around ten years – to iron out fluctuations. Data from *International Monetary Statistics Yearbooks,* Washington D: IMF and *100 Years of Economic Statistics* by Thelma Liesner.

*NB the Gross Investment figure for the USA for the period 1939 to 1944 covers private investment only, so the average Social Rate of Return for the US economy as a whole must have been lower than 164%.*

Worse is to come. Homing in on where our investment goes, only 2.7% of GDP - down 25% from 3.6% in 2008 - goes towards the most productive forms of investment, reasonably accurately covered by the Office for National Statistics (ONS) heading for "Other machinery and equipment".[4] In practice this is investment clustered round mechanisation, technology and power. Table 1.1 shows just how critical this is. Most investment – in road, rail, schools, hospitals, public buildings and housing in the public sector, and in office blocks, shopping centres, new restaurants and IT support services in the private sector – produces total returns of little more than the interest charges needed to finance them, as the very low figure for the UK in the table shows. The reason why countries such as China and Singapore grow so much faster than we do is that they spend far more on the much higher-powered investment in terms of returns - machinery, technology and power.

These types of investment are capable of producing much higher total returns. – often referred to in aggregate as the social rate of return - than is the case with almost all others. Think of a combine-harvester replacing a sickle, a large truck instead of a wheelbarrow, a computer replacing a multiplication table or a new machine producing twice as much as the one it replaces with the same inputs. Investment of this high-powered sort can and does achieve social rates of return which are far higher, as the figures in Table 1.1 show. The returns come back to the economy in a variety of different ways - as higher wages and salaries, better and often cheaper products, higher profits and a bigger tax base.

The average figures in the table are made up of a mixture of low returns on social investment and much higher returns from machinery, technology and power. To produce the average social rates of return achieved by Japan in the 1950s and 1960s – and China nowadays - they must be achieving total returns on these types of very highly productive investment of at least 50% per annum – and often more.

The problem with the UK is that the 2.7% of GDP which we spend on these types of investment is far too low to increase the stock of high-powered investment needed to push up our average social rate of return anywhere near the 14% world average, let alone the levels reached in really fast-growing economies. This is why we have a chronic productivity problem. But why, is Investment in the UK as a percentage of GDP – and particularly the most high-powered – so low? It is because its natural home is in the internationally tradable light industrial sector, which unfortunately has been chronically unprofitable, clearly exemplified by the fact that we have deindustrialised to the extent we have.

Typically for manufacturing operations, about one third of total costs are machinery, raw materials and components, for which there are world prices. The other two thirds are made up of direct labour and overhead costs, including interest and a provision for taxation.[5] All these costs are incurred in the domestic currency – sterling of course in our case – and are then charged out to the rest of the world, via the exchange rate.

## Table 1.2 Chained Real Effective Exchange Rates 1975-2017

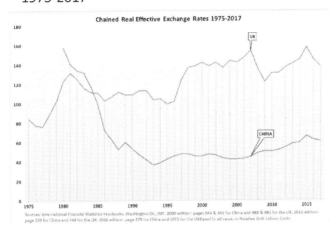

Chained Real Effective Exchange Rates 1975-2017

Sources: International Financial Statistics Yearbooks, Washington DC, IMF, 2000 edition: pages 344 & 345 for China and 980 & 981 for the UK, 2010 edition: page 229 for China and 744 for the UK; 2018 edition: page 279 for China and 1055 for the UK Based in all cases on Relative Unit Labour Costs

Most manufacturing output – especially the medium- and low-tech variety – is very price sensitive internationally and the key problem for the UK is that the exchange rate is too high for most UK manufactured output to be competitive. The graph above in Table 1.2 shows what has happened to sterling's competitiveness *vis à vis* China since the late-1970s when, even then, UK manufacturing was none too internationally competitive. It has been a combination of very high interest rates and tight money in the 1980s followed by the liberalisation and encouragement of capital imports in the 2000s, which between them pushed up the exchange rate to something like double its previous level, and which has been directly responsible for the collapse of UK industry.

The UK service sector and high-tech manufacturing are both relatively price-insensitive. Furthermore, services benefit to a substantial degree from natural advantages we have in our language, our geography, our legal system, our universities and the characteristics of our labour force.

Unfortunately, none of these advantages apply to manufacturing. This is why services can live happily with an exchange rate of perhaps $1.50 to the pound, while manufacturing needs a far lower rate – something like parity between sterling and the dollar. This is the crucial UK problem.

## Deindustrialisation

As recently as 1970, nearly a third of UK GDP came from manufacturing.[6] Now, it is less than 10%.[7] The conventional wisdom is that the decline of manufacturing is inevitable and does not matter very much. The contention in this book is that neither of these propositions is true. On the contrary, maintaining a reasonably substantial manufacturing base is critically important for at least four overlapping reasons.

### Table 1.3 - Growth, Manufacturing and Investment as a percentage of GDP in Various Countries

| | China | Korea | Sing-pre | Germany | Holland | USA | UK |
|---|---|---|---|---|---|---|---|
| %Growth in GDP 2006-2016 | 136 | 39 | 59 | 19 | 9 | 14 | 12 |
| %Growth in Population 2006/16 | 5.6 | 3.9 | 21.9 | 0.5 | 3.3 | 8.2 | 8.2 |
| %Growth in GDP per head 2006/16 | 124 | 33 | 30 | 19 | 6 | 5 | 3 |
| Manufacturing as a % of GDP | 29 | 29 | 20 | 23 | 12 | 12 | 10 |
| Investment as a % of GDP | 45 | 29 | 27 | 19 | 19 | 20 | 17 |

Sources: Various tables in *International Monetary Statistics Yearbook 2017*. Washington DC: IMF, 2017. Manufacturing data from the World Bank website. This data relates to 2016 as does the IMF data on Investment as a % of GDP.

First, productivity increases are much easier to achieve in manufacturing than they are in services, as Table 1.3 very strongly indicates. This is the case because manufacturing is the most natural home for mechanisation, technology and power – the critically important types of investment for increasing productivity. Economies with low percentage of GDP derived from manufacturing tend therefore to have relatively low growth rates, as the table shows.

Second, deindustrialisation has not affected all regions of the UK equally. Some were much more dependent on manufacturing than others before the decline in manufacturing as a percentage of GDP set in, and – hardly surprisingly - these have been far the most seriously hit by its decline. As a result, the most adversely affected regions have seen their percentages of GDP steadily falling. Between 2010 and 2016 the London economy grew by 22% net of inflation, while the North East managed only 4%. By 2016, GVA per head in London was 76% above the UK average and more than double that of 7 of the 11 remaining regions and countries of the UK.[8]

Third, understandably, the increase in regional GDP inequality is reflected in what has happened to real wages. Since 2007, real incomes in London have, on average, held their own. This is far from being the case in Wales and the North East, where the average real wage has fallen over the last 10 years respectively by 10% and 9%.[9] The result of London pulling away from the rest of the country is a huge and still increasing disparity in annual gross value added per employee. In 2015 this was £44k per head in London, £18k in Wales and £19k in the North East.[10]

Some of these huge disparities pre-tax are blunted by redistribution through the tax and benefit system, so that disposable incomes are not as sharply different as gross value added, but the consequence has been to make the regions more and more dependent on redistributive taxation and benefits, grants, loans and the sale of assets, at least partially to close the gap. London, reinforced by services, can hold its own in the world, but much of rest of the country is dependent on grants, and subsidies of various kinds for well over 10% of their living standards, which are still much lower than those in London.

Fourth, the collapse of so much of the country's manufacturing industry has left the UK with far too little to sell to the rest of the world to enable it to pay its way. Although services make up about 80% of the UK economy, in 2018 they provided no more than 45% of our export earnings. Manufacturing, comprising less than 10% of GDP supplied another 44%, with the balance being made up from raw materials and commodities such as oil.[11] Because services are generally much more difficult to sell abroad in sufficient quantities than services, if the UK's balance of payments gap is ever going to be closed – or at least reduced to manageable proportions – this will have to be done by the UK increasing its export of manufactures.

To rebalance our economy, we need to increase manufacturing as a percentage of GDP from its present barely 10% to around 15%. We do not need to emulate the 20% ratio achieved by countries such as Germany, Singapore and Switzerland because we have such a successful services export sector, which makes a balance of payments contribution on its own every year of some 5% of GDP.

# Balance of Payments

Table 1.4 shows what has happened to the UK's balance of payments over the past dozen years, from which a number of key conclusions can be drawn..

## Table 1.4 - UK Balance of Payments Breakdown – Net Figures in £bn

| Year | Goods Balance | Services Balance | Trade Balance | Net Income | Net Transfers | Balance of Payments |
|------|------|------|------|------|------|------|
| 2007 | -88.6 | 53.6 | -35 | -7.2 | -13.1 | -55.3 |
| 2008 | -91.7 | 52.7 | -39 | -14.6 | -13.2 | -66.8 |
| 2009 | -85.3 | 57.0 | -28.3 | -11.5 | -14.8 | -54.6 |
| 2010 | -95.6 | 60.5 | -35.1 | 1.1 | -19.6 | -53.6 |
| 2011 | -94.4 | 75.9 | -18.5 | 6.5 | -20.3 | -32.2 |
| 2012 | -106.7 | 81.1 | -25.6 | -17.8 | -20.4 | -63.8 |
| 2013 | -119.0 | 90.0 | -29.0 | -36.4 | -25.3 | -90.7 |
| 2014 | -122.1 | 92.4 | -29.7 | -37.8 | -23.4 | -93.2 |
| 2015 | -117.8 | 90.8 | -27.0 | -43.0 | -23.2 | -93.2 |
| 2016 | -132.7 | 101.8 | -30.9 | -49.4 | -22.5 | -102.8 |
| 2017 | -137.0 | 113.1 | -23.9 | -23.6 | -20.9 | -68.4 |

Source: Time Series Dataset. London: ONS, December 2018

First, while we have had a steadily deteriorating balance of trade on goods, this has been largely and successfully offset by our rising surplus on services, thus reducing the impact of our increasing lack of competitiveness on visible trade. Because the goods deficit is much larger than the services surplus, however, this has still left us with an overall trade deficit, albeit one which has been reasonably stable and of manageable size. The problem is that our overall balance of payments deficit has been much bigger than our trade deficit because a relatively small trade gap only makes up about one third of our total foreign payments deficit.

The second component of our balance of payments is our net income from abroad. This is made up very largely by the balance between what we get paid from abroad on our investments overseas and what investors in the UK receive in returns on their investments in the UK. Here there are obvious signs of marked deterioration. The main underlying reason for this is the cumulative effect of our having an overall balance of payments deficit year after year. This has to be financed by a combination of net sales of UK assets and borrowing from abroad, both of which involve cumulatively increasing negative net income streams. The inevitable result is that the net income balance tends to worsen.

Furthermore, the higher the exchange rate, the worse the income balance tends to be. This is because our foreign earnings are largely paid in world currencies while the returns on foreign investment within the UK are mostly paid in sterling. It is easy then to see that, the stronger the pound, the worse the net balance will tend to be. This effect is particularly pronounced because there are very large aggregate values – of the order of $15trn[12] - in both the value of UK investments overseas and foreign investment in the UK. The net figure is then the difference between two large totals, meaning that a change in the value of the pound makes a disproportionately large difference to the net figure.

The third component of our overseas balance is the net position on transfers abroad. About half of these are currently our net contribution to the EU budget, with the remainder split roughly equally between our overseas aid programmes and net remittances abroad by migrants to the UK. As the table shows, these have been on a slowly rising trend.

Since 2000, the cumulative value of the UK's balance deficit has been close to £1trn.[13] To finance this very substantial sum, which is equal to about half our annual GDP, not only have we had to borrow large sums from abroad; we have also sold off huge swathes of our national assets. These include most of our ports and airports, our football clubs, our power and utility companies, billions of pounds worth of residential and commercial properties, and much else. An ONS report produced in 2014 showed that by then as much as 29% of UK annual gross value added was generated by foreign owned companies.[14]

To a degree, most people would agree that it does not matter that much who owns our companies or even our housing, as long as it is well managed and used productively. But pushed beyond a certain point, this line of argument has to become suspect. It does matter if more and more of our economy is owned abroad by people who inevitably are going to put their home countries' interests before ours, who are going to concentrate their research and development activities near their head offices, who are going to pay most of their taxes to their home countries, and who may well divide up world markets in ways which may not suit us. Ever since 1999, when the Monopolies and Mergers Commission was abolished, to be replaced by the Competition Commission and the 2002 Enterprise Act,[15] unlike almost any other country in the world, we have had no public interest test which has to be passed before major take-overs of UK companies can take place. The result has been that we have lost control of large sectors of our economy, while the City earned an estimated £50bn in fees and charges over the years between 2000 and now from the sale of UK assets.[16] The resulting inflow of capital pushed up the value of the pound to a point where our manufacturing industry has been decimated and we cannot pay our way in the world.

## Borrowing and Lending

It is an accounting identity that - in any economy and indeed across world - all borrowing has to be exactly matched by equal lending and all surpluses have to be matched by equal but opposite deficits. Unfortunately, our policy-makers seem to have lost sight of both the inevitability of these relationships and their practical implications.

A key example relates to the deficits run up by the government year after year. As Table 1.5 shows, there is a strong relationship between government borrowing and the balance of payments. This arises because the impact of a foreign payments deficit is to siphon demand out of the economy as net payments go to foreign suppliers. This deficit has to be matched by excess spending over income – i.e. by borrowing -  somewhere ese in the economy. Some of the slack may be taken up by either the Household or the Corporate sectors – or both – but their net impact has never been anything like sufficiently large to offset the correlation between government borrowing and the foreign payments deficit.

## Table 1.5 - UK Net Lending (+) and Net Borrowing (-) by Sector in £bn

| Year | Public Sector | Corpor-ations | House-holds | Rest of World | Totals |
|------|------|------|------|------|------|
| 2008 | 81.9 | 13.9 | 29.2 | 66.5 | 0.0 |
| 2009 | -159.4 | 23.3 | 81.6 | 54.4 | -0.1 |
| 2010 | -147.8 | 10.0 | 83.4 | 54.3 | -0.1 |
| 2011 | -122.8 | 31.8 | 57.7 | 33.0 | -0.3 |
| 2012 | -136.8 | 10.6 | 62.6 | 64.4 | 0.9 |
| 2013 | -94.1 | -43.1 | 44.9 | 91.9 | -0.4 |
| 2014 | -98.8 | -38.7 | 44.9 | 92.8 | 0.2 |
| 2015 | -80.0 | -73.8 | 59.2 | 95.1 | 0.5 |
| 2016 | -57.6 | -63.3 | 16.8 | 104.5 | 0.4 |
| 2017 | -37.6 | -17.1 | -24.4 | 70.1 | -29.0 |

Source: Time Series data supporting ONS Quarterly National Accounts 2018 Q4. London: ONS, December 2018. Figures for 2017 are still being reconciled by ONS and the net totals will also be at or very close to zero when this process is complete.

This relationship, however, has profound policy implications. The thrust of government policy since the 2008 crash has been to reduce the government's deficit by a combination of cutting expenditure and increasing taxation. Leaving the Household and Corporate sectors on one side, this policy can only work if the foreign payments deficit is reduced pro rata. There is, however, no reason – at least directly - why this should happen. The foreign payment deficit is driven overwhelmingly by the factors exemplified in Table 1.4, and not by what happens – at least directly – by government decisions over axing and spending. This is clearly the way causation goes.

Could the government really not reduce its deficit by cutting expenditure and raising taxation? Yes, it could but only by doing what happened in Greece. There, the government deficit was eliminated, but only by depressing the whole economy by about 25% in real terms,[17] to such an extent that imports were reduced enough for them to be covered by exports. It was not prudent government management of its finances which got the Greek budget back in balance. It was plunging the economy into such a large depression that the foreign payments position was forced back into balance.

The crucial lesson to be learnt from this experience is that balancing the government's books without depressing the economy can only be done via policies which work directly on improving the balance of payments. This is why austerity policies – cutting expenditure and raising taxes – are an extremely inefficient and socially destructive way of cutting government borrowing. They only work by depressing the whole economy to improve the foreign payment balance. Essentially, this has to be the way in which austerity policies reduce government borrowing.

Excessive borrowing by either the government or consumers is not, however, the only debt problem. There is also a major international dimension to it, particularly for the UK and the USA. Both have run very large balance of payments deficits for a long time and have thus moved from being major creditors to being increasingly large-scale debtors. Meanwhile other countries have run up surpluses, as Table 1.6 shows.

**Table 1.6** Total Assets Minus Total Liabilities - Selected Countries - Ranked in Order of Net Balances to GDP. All Figures are in Billions of US dollars

| Country | Year | Total Assets | Total Liabilities | Net Balance | GDP | Ratio net assets to GDP |
|---------|------|--------------|-------------------|-------------|-----|-------------------------|
| Switz-erland | 2017 | 4,889 | 4,889 | 4,019 | 870 | 1.28 |
| Sing-apore | 2016 | 3,150 | 3,150 | 2,854 | 296 | 1.02 |
| Ger-many | 2017 | 10,009 | 7,696 | 2,313 | 3,678 | 0.63 |
| Japan | 2016 | 8,444 | 5,565 | 2,879 | 4,795 | 0.60 |
| China | 2016 | 6,507 | 4,557 | 1,950 | 11,040 | 0.18 |
| Russia | 2017 | 1,341 | 1,073 | 268 | 1,572 | 0.17 |
| S. Korea | 2016 | 1,454 | 1,205 | 249 | 1,449 | 0.17 |
| UK | 2017 | 14,386 | 14,738 | -352 | 2,622 | -0.13 |
| India | 2016 | 608 | 1,043 | -435 | 2,332 | -0.19 |
| Italy | 2017 | 3,028 | 3,366 | -338 | 1,793 | -0.19 |
| France | 2017 | 7,930 | 8,483 | -553 | 2,375 | -0.23 |
| Brazil | 2017 | 862 | 1,550 | -688 | 1,658 | -0.41 |
| U.S.A. | 2016 | 23,849 | 32,107 | -8,258 | 17,348 | -0.48 |
| Spain | 2017 | 2,248 | 3,376 | -1,128 | 1,173 | -0.96 |
| Greece | 2017 | 239 | 539 | -300 | 197 | -1.52 |
| Ireland | 2017 | 6,030 | 6,571 | -541 | 210 | - 2.58 |

Source: Country Tables in *International Financial Statistics Yearbook* Washington DC: IMF, 2018

The danger here is that the trust on which the financing of these huge debtor and creditor position requires will break down as the sums of money involved reach levels which are clearly unrepayable. It is not just the UK which needs to get its foreign payments position under much better control. The world has a major problem caused by some countries running unsustainably large deficits every year, matched by other countries with surpluses which could drag the whole world into the next recession.

## Inequality

Attaining complete equality between everyone is an impossible target. There are, nevertheless, reasonable differences of opinion held by people as to how wide the gaps should be between those with the greatest advantages and those who are not so lucky. Different sections of the electorate have varying views as do the political parties which represent different interests, which is why democracies can live with reasonable disparities of income and wealth. It helps, however, to have a reasonably contented and stable society if two conditions are fulfilled. One is that income, wealth and life chances are not too widely dispersed and the other is if the economy is growing fast enough for nearly everyone to feel that their real incomes are increasing. The problem in the UK at present is that the first of these conditions is arguably no longer being fulfilled. while the second is demonstrably not being achieved.

The most commonly used measure of the overall degree in inequality is the Gini coefficient. This would be 0 if everyone had the same income and 1 if one person had everything and everyone else nothing. By this measure, as Table 1.7 shows, the UK became much more unequal during the Thatcher ern and since then, except for a peak running up to the 2008 crash, has stayed roughly stable.

## Table 1.7 Income share over time

Income share over time

Gini Coefficient 1961 - 2015/16

Since the 1990s, changes inequality have been less dramatic than the change from 1979 t0 1991. After falling slightly in the early to mid 1990s, inequality as shown by the Gini coefficient, reached a new peak of 0.385 in 2009-10. Inequality fell in 2010 and has stayed relatively level since.

Table 1.8 then shows what has happened to nominal and real wages over the period since just before the 2008 crash.

# Table 1.8 Average Weekly Earnings total pay: real and nominal, whole economy, seasonally adjusted 2015=100 January 2005 to June 2018 Great Britain

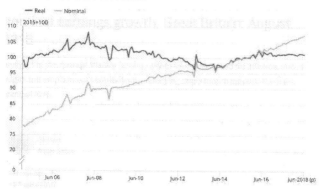

Source: Monthly Wages and Salaries Survey, Office for National Statistics

Inequality in the UK has a multiplicity of different dimensions, especially between different regions of the country, between varying generations and between different socio-economic groups. Until the 1970s, average living standards were higher in the North of England than they were in the South.[18] Now this position has been comprehensively reversed.

After the impact of taxation and expenditure has been taken into account, actual disparities in living standards within the regions – although still very considerable - were not so marked, but only because of huge net transfers from the South East to the rest of the country.

Between the generations born during the first 25 years after World War II and those whose life started since 1990, again there are huge contrasts between the opportunities which they have encountered in education, housing, incomes and job opportunities.

Whereas the 1945-1970 cohort had free tertiary education, the 1990 onwards one has had to borrow £9,000 a year to help to pay for this privilege. Those who bought houses and flats before around 1980 have been the beneficiaries of very large real increases in the value of their properties, making it at the same time more and more difficult for younger people to get started on the housing ladder. The UK has a flexible labour force, which is one of the main reasons why unemployment is so low, but these favourable figures belie the fact that over a quarter of jobs in the UK are not full time and often not sufficiently secure to be properly protected by employment legislation.[19]

As regards income, wealth and all the life chances which are associated with it, Table 1.9 shows what has happened over the last few years. The top 0.1% saw their incomes far more than doubling up to the time of the 2008 crash, but still settling down to about twice what they were in the early 1990s. At the other end of the scale, the whole of the bottom 90% of income earners have experienced no real increases at all for nearly two decades. At a time when the FTSE 100 CEOs receive on average annual income of £5.3 a year – 386 times the income of someone earning the national minimum wage, 165 times more than the average nurse, 140 times more than teachers and 132 times more than police officers[20] – a higher and higher proportion of the population depends on food banks.

# Table 1.9 Income Growth at the Top

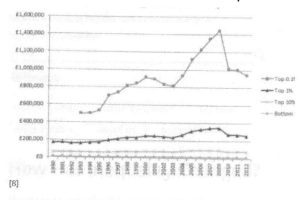

Legend:
- Top 0.1%
- Top 1%
- Top 10%
- Bottom

[8]

Notes: Income is gross income and measured at the individual level.

The issue here is not how can we achieve equality of incomes for everyone.   It is how can we avoid the disparities becoming so wide that the country's social fabric starts to break down. Everyone has an interest in making sure that this does not happen – and it is our sluggish growth rate and our lopsided and unbalanced economy which is largely responsible for these excessive and unsustainable inequality trends which we urgently need to constrain - and hopefully redress.

## Notes

1. ONS code NPQT minus EQDO divided by YBHA. London: ONS 2018
2. Consumption of fixed capital in the UK in 2016 was 12.9% of GDP. Page 829 in International Financial Statistics Yearbook 2017. Washington DC: IMF 2017
3. Page 829 in *International Financial Statistics Yearbook 2018.* Washington DC: IMF, 2018
4. ONS code DLWO divided by YBHA. London: ONS, 2018
5. Page 7 in *Economic Review* March 2014. London: ONS 2014
6. www.economicshelp.org/blog/7617/economics

7.  Calculations based n ONS codes ABMI and YBEX. London: ONS December 2017

8.  House of Commons Briefing Paper 05795, dated 5th September 2018

9.  Calculated from ONS NUTS data.

10. ONS Regional GVA Income Approach. London: ONS 2016

11. ONS codes BOKI, IKBB, BOPO and BOPP

12. PE 1057 IN *International Financial Statistics Yearbook.* Washington DC: IMF 2018.

13. Times Series Data Set for ONS code HBOP

14. Report in *The Guardian* 11th September 2014

15. Wikipedia entry on the 2002 Enterprise Act

16. Calculate s 3% of the gross value of the transactions involved.

17. Page 88 in *International Statistics Yearbook 2017.* Washington DC: IMF 2017

18. Poverty and wealth across Britain 1968 to 2005. ERF website

19. UK February2019 Labour Market Report. London, ONS, 2019 2019

20. Data from The Equality, Trust website.

# Chapter 2

# Solutions

What can be done to overcome all these problems – to reduce their scale and impact and, where possible, to get them reversed? What are the components of the strategy we require to tackle systematically the root causes of what is wrong with our economy and what we need to do to put things right? The approach which needs to be adopted has a number of different elements. It has to involve a review of our economic priorities, to make sure that our policies are as rationally ordered as possible. It entails reconsideration of where we need to get the stimulus to come from to allow economic growth to take place on a sustainable basis. It needs to see how we can remould many of the well-canvassed supply side remedies for our economic condition, to see how much more effective their contribution could be if it was accompanied by demand side reform. It needs to tackle the difficulties there would be in transitioning to a considerably faster rate of growth than we have achieved recently. And it needs to consider carefully the objections which are likely to be raised to the radical change of strategy proposed in this book, and how they can be overcome.

Here is what needs to be done.

## Neoliberalism

First, there needs to be a much more sceptical and effective challenge than is common at the moment to the mostly uncritical view taken about the neoliberal consensus on which economic policy making in the UK very largely depends. Neoliberalism was an understandable response to the inflationary problems of the 1970s and 1980s, but in key respects, it has now run its course.

The period of relatively successful growth in the UK economy which took place during the first quarter of a century after the end of world War II came to an end after 1971 with the break-up of the Bretton Woods post-war settlement. Relieved of the policy constraints which the Bretton Woods system entailed, there was a very substantial expansion of the money supply, leading to a large but short-lived boom across the world. The world economy expanded by 4.7% in 1971 and 6.6% in 1972[1] before falling back into stagnation accompanied by very rapid price increases which peaked, year on year, in the UK at almost 25%.[2] Excess demand was undoubtedly largely to blame – transmitted partly by huge increases in commodity prices. Most doubled while the price of oil rose from $2.50 to $10.00 dollars a barrel.[3] Understandably, in these circumstances getting inflation under control became top priority. The Keynesian policy framework, which had underpinned the prosperity of previous decades had no convincing response to the inflationary crisis. As a result, there was a very rapid switch towards a very different policy approach in the form of monetarism, which subsequently morphed into the neoliberalism which still prevails.

Monetarists claimed that inflation could be tamed by an apparently simple – albeit radical - policy change. This was to allow the money supply only to increase by a target amount made up of real growth plus whatever level of inflation was deemed acceptable. In practice, it meant monetary restraint and steep rises in interest rates, with base rates peaking at 17%[4] in the UK and 20%[5] in the USA.

These policies did reduce inflation – although the extent to which price increases would have moderated anyway is disputed – but with very significant side-effects. The most important of these was a huge increase exchange rates, particularly among the countries – primarily the UK and the USA - which put these new policies into effect most assiduously. The exact relationships posited by monetarism turned out not to exist but containing inflation as top economic priority persisted, as 2% inflation targets, which entailed relatively restrictive economic measures, kept exchange rates up.

The UK then compounded the impact on the exchange rate of neoliberal high interest rate policies in the 1980s to combat inflation with capital liberalisation which led to enormous capital inflows in the 1990s and especially the 2000s, driving the pound up to its $2.00 parity peak in 2007.[6] This all happened at a time when many economies along the Pacific Rim were devaluing their currencies. The result was the huge loss of competitiveness shown in Table 1.2 on page 5. This is the fundamental reason why the UK – and many other western economies – have deindustrialised to the extent they have. It is why our manufacturing base - unable to compete with anything like such an uncompetitive exchange rate - has become so attenuated. This is why our output per hour and our growth rate have slowed up as much as they have; why we cannot pay our way in the world; why we are borrowing so much; why the inequalities within our economy have become so marked. And why, in summary, our economy has become so unbalanced.

The crucial significance of these highly adverse trends is that they ought to have triggered a shift in economic policy objectives. Unfortunately, this has not happened. Despite the enormous increases in the monetary base in recent years, inflation has receded as a problem, but trying to control it is still the primary aim of economic policy. While this has been happening, growth, investment and competitiveness have all lost salience as policy targets. Of course, keeping inflation under control is important but raising living standards and taking steps to rebalance the economy are much more crucial objectives.

## Demand

It is a truism to say that the UK economy will only be able to grow more quickly if demand for what it is capable of producing rises more rapidly than it has done recently. The problem in the UK is that such increases in demand as there have been have tended to come from the wrong sources for sustainability. As Table 1.5 shows, they have come mainly from consumers - much of it from borrowing - and from government expenditure being greater than its revenue. Instead, we need to get much more coming from investment – especially in the most productive types in terms of productivity growth – and net trade, i.e. exports minus imports.

Specifically, we need to get the economy rebalanced onto a footing which will enable it to expand sustainably at between 3% and 4% annum. This is the rate needed both to stop us sliding down the world rankings, which is bound to happen if we grow more slowly than the world average. It is also about the rate required to secure real income increases for most of the population. To achieve this change, we need to have two key targets. First, we need to get the proportion of our GDP which we invest in our future every year up from its current barely 16% to something like 25% - close to the world average. Second, we need to get the proportion of our GDP devoted to manufacturing up from under 10% to around 15%. This is a lower ratio than the 20% or so achieved by many successful economies such as Germany, Switzerland and Singapore, but these economies lack the service sector balance of payments surplus generated by the UK, which – on its own – is about 5% of our GDP.[7] The key issue, then, is how to engineer these transitions. The answer is to use the price incentives provided by a much more competitive exchange rate.

The rationale for this approach is that the only way of both getting our rate of investment and the proportion of our GDP devoted to manufacturing up to the extent required is to generate strong enough price and financial signals to get the necessary changes made. This means making it much more profitable to manufacture in the UK compared to elsewhere than it is now, because this is where productivity increase are most easily secured. We have to increase the overall percentage of GDP devoted both to investment and to manufacturing. We need to make it more profitable to site new production facilities – across the widest possible range of high- medium- and low-tech manufacturing – in the UK rather than elsewhere in the world.

How low would the exchange rate need to be to get these conditions fulfilled? Estimates taking careful account of the price sensitivities involved indicate that we would need rough parity between the pound and the dollar and around £1.00 = €0.85.

This is clearly a far lower exchange rate than the one broadly required for services which have done well for the UK with an exchange rate of $1.50 to the dollar or more. The problem is that the UK evidently cannot pay its way in the world, based on our record of successful service sector exports, on their own. To reduce our foreign payments deficit to manageable proportions, we need a much more substantial net trade contribution from somewhere else, and the only conceivable alternative is from manufacturing for which, with none of our service sector's natural advantages – an exchange rate of $1.50 to £1.00 is lethal.

A key component of this strategy is that we should no longer aim to keep relying on more and more sophisticated and high-tech manufacturing to maintain our share of world trade. Of course, we should encourage as much as we can our most sophisticated  industries, but we should also realise that there are never going to be enough high-tech manufacturing opportunities to provide the total export volumes and value we need.  Instead we should follow the lead provided by advanced countries such as Holland and Germany, with very successful export records based on producing large volumes of high-quality medium- and low-tech products at competitive prices.  It is highly significant, for example, that less than 20% of German exports are high-tech.[8] The only way for us to produce enough to pay our way in the world is to have a sufficiently broadly-based industrial base to enable us to do so.

## Supply

Concern about the relatively mediocre performance of the UK economy has prompted numerous efforts in recent years to explain what might have gone wrong and to propose remedies. The vast majority of this work has been carried out within broadly the neoliberal policy framework, which assumes that an exchange rate strategy is not an option. This is mainly because such a policy is not thought to be compatible with the over-riding priority given by neoliberalism to price stability. The outcome has then been broadly two approaches. On the right of centre, it has been to promote a better economic growth record by using deregulation, privatisation, low taxation, freer markets and a smaller role for the state as triggers for better performance. On the left, there has been heavy emphasis on supply side strategies, focusing on such issues as better education and training, less short-termism, better governance, tax incentives to encourage capital expenditure, more public sector investment, devolution of responsibility for economic decisions from the centre to the regions, and easier access to finance for industry.

The fact that all these ideas have been common currency for years while growth in the economy has been in secular decline points to their ineffectiveness – unless accompanied by corresponding demand-side changes which would create the condition in which the remedies of both the right and the left would have important and constructive roles to contribute, In the absence of any demand side changes, however, most of the deficiencies highlighted by both the right and the left are much more the consequences than the causes of slow growth. Implementing any of these supply side measures on their own will not therefore do anything significant to improve the UK's economic performance and its growth rate.

This is not to deny that there is an important role, as right of centre thinkers say, for markets in allocating resources efficiently; that excessive regulation and crony capitalism are a drag on economic performance, that the private sector can run some services better than the public sector or that excessively high rates of taxation can act as a disincentive to innovation. The problem is that dealing with all these factors, even if taken together, would not make that much difference to the economy's performance and, even if they did, most of their improvement would be "one off" rather than providing substantially better performance year after year.

Similar criticism is easy to level at supply side agendas from the left. Improved education and training are only worthwhile if opportunities for using increased skills are there to be exploited, otherwise all the effort and expense goes to waste. Short-termism and share buy-backs are not irrational if there are no profitable investment opportunities. Tax reliefs on profits only work if there are profits on which tax can be reduced   Public sector capital investment generally has low social rates of return and therefore contributes little directly to economic growth, however, desirable it may be from a social point of view. There is little sign that the devolution agenda has produced significant growth outcomes. More finance for industry will only help if, again here are profitable opportunities to be exploited.

What all this is telling us however, is not that all these supply side remedies proposed by both the right and left of centre have nothing to contribute.  On the contrary, almost all would have a positive role to play if married to a combined approach involving both demand and supply side reform adopted at the same time. We need efficient markets and all the benefits which better designed tax system could bring.in train. We also need all the benefits which the industrial strategy agenda could contribute. We need, as well, to provide a reasonable balance between enhanced social provision and economic advancement and – not least – to ensure that there are adequate resources for the green agenda and that adequate attention is paid to ecological sustainability.

There is one particular supply-side change which could make a big difference.  This is to make sure that in future it is very easy – instead of generally extremely difficult - to obtain finance for new or expanding industrial projects. This means changing the role of banks in the UK from devoting most of their loans to purchase of property and personal lending to giving much more focus to financing manufacturing on the softest possible terms. This would probably require some form of public guarantee to ensure that the risks involved in a strategy such as this were shared out in a manageable way. There is an important model for this kind of policy approach in what Japan did after World War II, generating the huge volume of highly productive investment which – along with a highly competitive exchange rate! - led to their 10% per annum growth rate in the early decades after World War II.

There is also a general point to be made about the quality of UK manufacturing management, which – although there are important exceptions - leaves a great deal to be desired. The low profitability and poor social status of manufacturing in the UK, compared to other professions, has led to many manufacturing companies being run by people who are not of comparable ability to those with which they must compete in international markets. One of the key requirements, if there is to be a renaissance of UK manufacturing, is that we need to create an environment which attracts in a new cadre of highly capable entrepreneurs to the business of making and selling British products. Provided there is money to be made, there is no evidence at all that such people would not materialise - and be employed far more productively than in other ways in which they might otherwise be engaged.

## Objections

A common reaction to the proposals which this book sets out is to dismiss them out of hand as impractical and unworkable. This is in striking contrast to the attitudes in many other countries – such as Germany, Switzerland, Singapore, China and South Korea, all with much better economic growth records over the years than ours - where exchange rate policy and mainlining international competitiveness are top of their policy agendas. What persuades people in the UK that the exchange rate does not matter – or can't be changed? There are six main arguments which are regularly advanced. Five can relatively easily be countered while one – to do with inflation – is potentially more substantial and is covered in the next section.

First, it is alleged that, in a relatively open economy such as ours, the exchange rate is determined entirely by market forces, over which the authorities have no control. Of course, market sentiment affects the day to day value of the pound, but it is completely untrue that this stops the authorities and the government having very substantial influence over the exchange rate if they are minded to do so – as indeed is clearly the case with currency management in many other parts of the world. On the contrary, there is plenty the government could to get the pound down if it was determined to get this done.

It could announce a major change in exchange rate policy, explaining why it was being adopted. It could make it obvious to everyone that going for a competitive exchange rate was a strategic policy initiative, not least by making it clear that it would become a major plank of government policy to make sure it was sustained. It could instruct the Bank of England to sell sterling to get the pound down, rather than leaving the Bank with no exchange rate policy objective, as is the case at present, but inclined to favour a relatively high rate in the hope that this will hold down inflation. It could restrict capital inflows, which drive up the value of sterling, using tax policy to make it less attractive for overseas investors to buy UK assets. It could make it more difficult – as is done by almost all other countries - for foreign interests to buy UK companies and other portfolio assets. Major changes in currency valuations have been engineered before by government action – for example the Plaza Accord in 1985.[9] There is no reason why this could not happen again.

Second, would there be a problem about retaliation and what should we do about the fact that we have given commitments to the G7 and others that the UK will not engage in exchange rate manipulation to gain an unfair advantage? Here, we need to recognise what a disadvantaged and unsustainable situation we have as our starting point, especially if we take a medium- to long-term point of view.

The problem is that there have never been effective enough ways of bringing pressure on countries with low and highly competitive exchange rates – and with consequent foreign payments surpluses – to revalue their currencies to bring international trade back into reasonable balance. It should not be our policy to run a large balance of payments surplus, as happens – taking 2017 figures – in countries such as Holland (11.6% of GDP)[10] Germany (7.6%),[11] Saudi Arabia (6.1%)[12] and Singapore (26%!).[13] Instead we should aim to run a modest deficit. In the long-term, this will produce more stability than a probable crash sooner or later in the value of the pound as its over-valuation eventually spooks the markets.

Third, it is contended that reducing the value of the pound on the international exchanges will make us all poorer. Measured in US dollars or any other non-sterling currency, this will of course be true, but this is beside the point. UK consumers do not shop in foreign currency, except perhaps when they are on holiday. They shop in pounds and in this sense what Harold Wilson, then the Prime Minister, famously said in 1967 when the pound was devalued, was correct: "From now the pound abroad is worth 14 per cent or so less in terms of other currencies. It does not mean, of course, that the pound here in Britain, in our pocket or purse or in you bank, has been devalued".[14]

In fact, international GDP comparisons tend almost invariably to show the growth rate of countries which devalue going up faster than they did before. If this happens, as a matter of logic, real GDP per head of the population – far from going down - must also go up faster than it did previously. It is true, however, that faster growth tends to entail more investment and correspondingly less consumption, so that disposable incomes may be under some pressure. This is, nevertheless, an inevitable consequence of any strategy for increasing the growth rate. Furthermore, if the economy can be made to grow fast enough, higher GDP may offset a higher percentage of incomes going on investment rather than current spending, providing a win-win outcome.

Fourth, we are told that we have tried devaluation before and it doesn't work. As a matter of fact, it clearly is not true that when the pound has come down, there has been no improvement in our trade balance, certainly in relation to what it otherwise might have been. Even though the sensitivity of our export and import volumes to price changes has gone down recently, as all the most price sensitive parts of our economy have ben hollowed out by unmanageable competition, there was still some improvement in our foreign payment balance after the post-EU referendum devaluation as Table 1.4 shows. The real problem is that we have always left getting the pound down too late, and never devalued enough to make it worth re-establishing manufacturing industry in the UK.

Finally, there is a view that the UK is no good at manufacturing and should not try to hold its own in the world with exports of manufactured goods. This is surely both a counsel of despair and one which is totally at odds with our history and practical experience. Unless we envisage a future in which we go on selling national assets to finance a standard of living which we are not earning until eventually the markets turn against us and the pound crashes, we have no alternative but to export more and import less – and the only way in which we are going to be able to do this in sufficient volume is by selling more manufactures abroad and importing less. Services will never fill the gap because they ae too difficult to sell abroad in sufficient volume.

As to the contention that the British are no good at making and selling things, this only reflects the fact that in the UK it is so much harder to make money out of manufacturing than it is to prosper by following other careers. As a result, industry in the UK has been starved of talent for many decades. If the environment was changed to one where making money out of producing goods for export or import saving was highly profitable – as it is in all countries with competitive exchange rates – then there is no reason whatsoever for believing that a new breed of UK entrepreneurs would not appear in the UK to take advantage of the new opportunities. This is what happens everywhere when the right pricing signals – a clearly articulated policy to keep the exchange rate at a competitive level – are made to apply. Like them, the UK needs to use economic and price incentives to tempt its brightest people into running manufacturing companies – something which we have not done on nearly big enough scale for 200 years. Then we will see UK industry reviving - but without the right financial incentives, it never will.

## Transition

There is a well-trodden path by which advanced countries have allowed themselves to lose competitiveness, to deindustrialise, and to let their rate of economic growth slow up. This is the condition from which most of the West suffers, and there is really no example so far of this process being reversed. To undo this course in the UK is therefore going to involve covering new ground.

What are the hurdles which need to be overcome to make sure that this happens?

The first problem is to persuade enough politicians, academics, civil servants and the people who make up public opinion that there is a much better way ahead for our country than is at all likely to be achieved on present trends with the current neoliberal consensus. This is not going to be an easy task, not only because of the difficulties involved in getting any large number of people to change their minds, but also because most influential people are not particularly hard hit by the conditions in our economy which impact so adversely on many others. By and large, key opinion-formers enjoy high living standards and they and their families and friends are contented with their lot in life. The impact of low levels of investment, deindustrialisation, regional inequality, balance of payments deficits, and consumer and government borrowing on their personal lives is not very harsh and many rich people are more than content with the redistributive impact in their favour of neoliberal policies. The message from this book, however, is that nothing will materially change for the better until the realisation sinks in that the situation for a majority of the population is much worse than a lot of well-off people realise, as is all too clearly reflected in our current political discontents.

The second problem is the widely and firmly held view that devaluations always cause inflation and falling living standards because prices then rise faster than incomes. History, however, tells otherwise. Table 2.1 shows what happened following all the major downward movements of the UK exchange rate which have taken place since 1931. In 1931 and 1992, prices subsequently actually fell substantially. After 1949 and 1967 there were rises but mainly because of other factors – rearmament for the Korean War in 1950 and a rash of inflationary strikes in 1968. Increases in price rises after 2008 and 2016 were modest. There is no evidence here of runaway inflation or of the extra price competitiveness achieved as a result of lower exchange rates being washed away by more rapid price increase than could reasonably have been expected anyway.

In fact, there are good reasons why devaluations – both in the UK and elsewhere – do not produce much, if any, additional inflation or adverse effects on the real wage. While import prices must rise, this tends to be offset by other factors which bring price increases down – longer production runs, switches to now cheaper domestic suppliers from those overseas, lower interest and tax rates.

As to the argument that lower exchange rates adversely affect the real wage, because they almost universally generate faster growth, GDP per head as a matter of logic must go up. It is true, however, that if faster growth entails more investment, then more saving will be required, but this is true of any growth policy.

## Table 2.1

| Year of Devaluation | Overall Devaluation percentage | Inflation previous year | Inflation devaluation year | Inflation devaluation year + 1 | Inflation devaluation year + 2 | Inflation devaluation year +3 |
|---|---|---|---|---|---|---|
| 1931 | 25% | - 1.7% | -10.1% | -9.9% | -6.6% | +5.5% |
| 1949 | 31% | 5.1% | 2.4% | 2.7% | 9.9% | 6.3% |
| 1967 | 16% | 3.9% | 2.7% | 4.8% | 5.4% | 6.3% |
| 1992 | 15% | 5.9% | 3.7% | 1.6% | 2.5% | 3.4% |
| 2008 | 22% | 2.3% | 3.6% | 2.2% | 3.3% | 4.5% |
| 2016 | 9% | 0.1% | 1.3% | 2.6% | 2.4% | 1.9% |

Sources: *One Hundred Years of Economic Statistics* by Thelma Liesner. London: Facts on File and the Economist, 1989, and successive editions of *International Statistics Yearbook. Washington DC, IMF.* Combined with data from the Office for National Statistics and https//inflationdata.com

Leaving aside the need to ensure that inflation stays within reasonable bounds, there are in fact only two other critical conditions which have to be met to ensure that the outcome will be the transformation in growth projections which a competitive exchange strategy is designed to achieve. One is that the responsiveness of exports and imports – the elasticity of demand for them – is sufficiently great to avoid the foreign payment balance getting out of hand. The other is that the social rate of return on investment, if directed towards mechanisation, technology and power by the right price signals - will be of sufficient magnitude to generate the extra resources necessary to make the proposed policy work. Fortunately, there is ample evidence that both these key requirements can be met.

The evidence that the price sensitivity of UK exports and imports would be sufficiently high to get our foreign payments balance back under control if the exchange rate was sufficiently competitive comes both from world figures showing what the price sensitivity is generally for manufactured goods and from our own history. Recently the elasticity of demand for UK exports and imports does seem to have decreased substantially, but this is hardly surprising if nearly all our price sensitive manufacturing has been driven out of business. The key to this problem is to get the exchange rate down to a point where it is worth siting new manufacturing plant in the UK. This is what is needed to drive up the elasticities to where they need to be.

As to the full – or social – rate of return which can be achieved on investment – especially on machinery, technology and power - Table 1.1 shows clearly what can be achieved in the right circumstances. Since most of this investment takes place in the privately-owned tradable sectors of the economy, the key requirement to make it happen is profitability, which is what a competitive exchange rate will deliver. In essence, the way to get the UK economy to grow at about 3.5% per annum instead of 1.5% is to shift 4% of UK GDP out of consumption and into high powered investment which has a social rate of return of at least 50% a year. This will increase the growth rate by 4% x 50%, which is 2% per annum.

This is the strategy which will deliver sustainable growth for the UK economy at about the world's average rate.

## Notes

1.   Page 329 in *The world Economy: A Millennial Perspective* by Angus Maddison. Paris: OECD, 2001

2.  Page 59 in *International Monetary Statistics Yearbook 1979.* Washington DC: IMF, 1979
3.  Ibid, pages 74 to 81
4.  Bank of England website
5.  Federal Reserve website
6.  Page 806 in *International Monetary Statistics Yearbook 2014.* Washington DC: EMF 2014
7.  ONS code IKBD divided by ABMI
8.  Data provided by Policy Network
9.  Wikipedia entry on The Plaza Accord
10. Page 760 in *International Statistics Yearbook 2018.* Washington DC: IMF, 2018
11. Ibid, page 455
12. Ibid, page 891
13. Ibid, page 9
14. https:commonslibrary.parliament.uk

# Chapter 3

# Conclusion

For the past three years, Brexit has been a massive distraction to those thinking about the UK's underlying economic condition and what needs to be done about it. Whatever the final outcome of the current Brexit negotiations, the UK - sooner or later – is going to have to pay its way in the world and to stop relying on borrowing and selling assets every year to pay for a standard of living which we are not earning. In the shorter term we face the familiar highly divisive problems of lack of investment, deindustrialisation, foreign payments deficits, excessive borrowing and mounting inequality. Our economic problems are clearly a large part of the cause of the social and political discontent, which in turn are putting increasingly severe pressure on our cohesion as a country and the capacity of our democracy to take the strain.

There is thus a very urgent need to get policies implemented in the UK which will get our economy back into better balance and growing faster. The conclusions in this book are that there is little prospect of making any of this happen unless we can make our economy more competitive than it is at present, and that there is no other practical way of achieving this other than through a proactive competitive exchange rate strategy.

Like any other major policy change, however, a major upheaval like this carries risks. The evidence marshalled above strongly suggests that the values of the key metrics – on inflation, the sensitivity of our international trade to more competitive pricing and the total returns on investment of the most productive type - are all of the right orders of magnitude. The risk of failure is therefore relatively low.

And these risks need to be balanced against those which are very likely to materialise if we continue as we are. With our current levels and patterns of investment, the UK economy is very unlikely to grow as far ahead as we can see at more than about 1.5% per annum, of which around half will be pre-empted by population increase. In these circumstances, most people are going to receive no increase in real incomes for the foreseeable future while many will see a reduction in their standards of living as the better off manage to secure what little increases in the total income pot there are. We will forego any chance of reindustrialisation, with all the consequences this will bring in the form of foregone productivity improvements, lost job prospects, increasing imbalances between London and the regions and chronic balance of payments deficits. Borrowing and debts will rise and inequality will increase.

And it is not just that our economic prospects look so poor. It is our social conditions and our politics which will be in severe danger of suffering too. With growth almost at a standstill, the country will become more divided and our politics more fractious. Trust in the competence and trustworthiness of our ruling elite will erode. The UK will sink further and further down the world league table in terms of economic salience and influence. Our civilised and tolerant way of life may finish up being under threat if populism and extremism take over.

Whatever we do, we have some big risks to manage, and we need to make the right choices. A huge amount is at stake.

**Bite-Sized Public Affairs Books** are designed to provide insights and stimulating ideas that affect us all in, for example, journalism, social policy, education, government and politics.

They are deliberately short, easy to read, and authoritative books written by people who are either on the front line or who are informed observers. They are designed to stimulate discussion, thought and innovation in all areas of public affairs. They are all firmly based on personal experience and direct involvement and engagement.

The most successful people all share an ability to focus on what really matters, keeping things simple and understandable. When we are faced with a new challenge most of us need quick guidance on what matters most, from people who have been there before and who can show us where to start. As Stephen Covey famously said, "The main thing is to keep the main thing, the main thing."

But what exactly is the main thing?

Bite-Sized books were conceived to help answer precisely that question crisply and quickly and, of course, be engaging to read, written by people who are experienced and successful in their field.

The brief? Distil the 'main things' into a book that can be read by an intelligent non-expert comfortably in around 60 minutes. Make sure the book enables the reader with specific tools, ideas and plenty of examples drawn from real life. Be a virtual mentor.

We have avoided jargon – or explained it where we have used it as a shorthand – and made few assumptions about the reader, except that they are literate and numerate, involved in understanding social policy, and that they can adapt and use what we suggest to suit their own, individual purposes. Most of all the books are focused on understanding and exploiting the changes that we witness every day but which come at us in what seems an incoherent stream.

They can be read straight through at one easy sitting and then referred to as necessary – a trusted repository of hard-won experience.

## Bite-Sized Books Catalogue

## Business Books

Ian Benn
>	Write to Win
>>		How to Produce Winning Proposals and
>>		RFP Responses

Matthew T Brown
>	Understand Your Organisation
>>		An Introduction to Enterprise Architecture
>>		Modelling

David Cotton
>	Rethinking Leadership
>>		Collaborative Leadership for Millennials
>>		and Beyond

Richard Cribb
>	IT Outsourcing: 11 Short Steps to Success
>>		An Insider's View

Phil Davies
>	How to Survive and Thrive as a Project Manager
>>		The Guide for Successful Project
>>		Managers

Paul Davies
>	Developing a Business Case
>>		Making a Persuasive Argument out of
>>		Your Numbers

Paul Davies
>Developing a Business Plan
>>Making a Persuasive Plan for Your
>>Business

Paul Davies
>Contract Management for Non-Specialists

Paul Davies
>Developing Personal Effectiveness in Business

Paul Davies
>A More Effective Sales Team
>>Sales Management Focused on Sales
>>People

Paul Davies
>The Naked Human in Business
>>Accelerate Your Personal Effectiveness by
>>Understanding Humans – The Practical
>>One Two Three of Business Development

Tim Emmett
>Bid for Success
>>Building the Right Strategy and Team

Nigel Greenwood
>Why You Should Welcome Customer Complaints
>>And What to Do About Them

Nigel Greenwood
>Six Things that All Customer Want
>>A Practical Guide to Delivering Simply
>>Brilliant Customer Service

Stuart Haining
>The Practical Digital Marketeer – Volume 1
>>Digital Marketing – Is It Worth It and Your
>>First Steps

Stuart Haining

> The Practical Digital Marketeer – Volume 2
>> Planning for Success

Stuart Haining

> The Practical Digital Marketeer – Volume 3
>> Your Website

Stuart Haining

> The Practical Digital Marketeer – Volume 4
>> Be Sociable – Even If You Hate It

Stuart Haining

> The Practical Digital Marketeer – Volume 5
>> Your On-going Digital Marketing

Stuart Haining

> Profitable Partnerships
>> Practical Solutions to Help Pick the Right
>> Business Partner

Stuart Haining

> MLM 101
>> The Difficult Questions and Answers Most
>> Networkers Daren't Reveal

Christopher Hosford

> Great Business Meetings! Greater Business
> Results
>> Transforming Boring Time-Wasters into
>> Dynamic Productivity Engines

Ian Hucker

> Risk Management in IT Outsourcing
>> 9 Short Steps to Success

Alan Lakey

> Idiocy in Commercial Life
>> Practical Ways to Navigate through
>> Nonsense

Marcus Lopes and Carlos Ponce
　　Retail Wars
　　　　May the Mobile be with You
Maiqi Ma
　　Win with China
　　　　Acclimatisation for Mutual Success Doing
　　　　Business with China
Elena Mihajloska
　　Bridging the Virtual Gap
　　　　Building Unity and Trust in Remote Teams
Rob Morley
　　Agile in Business
　　　　A Guide for Company Leadership
Gillian Perry
　　Managing the People Side of Change
　　　　Ten Short Steps to Success in IT
　　　　Outsourcing
Art Rain
　　The Average Wage Millionaire
　　　　Can Anyone Really Get Rich?
Saibal Sen
　　Next Generation Service Management
　　　　An Analytics Driven Approach
Don Sharp
　　Nothing Happens Until You Sell Something
　　　　A Personal View of Selling Techniques

# Lifestyle Books

Anna Corthout
　　Alive Again
　　　　My Journey to Recovery

Anna Corthout
    Mijn Tweede Leven
        Kruistocht naar herstel
Phil Davies
    Don't Worry Be Happy
        A Personal Journey
Phil Davies
    Feel the Fear and Pack Anyway
        Around the World in 284 Days
Stuart Haining
    My Other Car is an Aston
        A Practical Guide to Ownership and Other
        Excuses to Quit Work and Start a Business
Stuart Haining
    After the Supercar
        You've Got the Dream Car – But Is It Easy
        to Part With?
Bill Heine
    Cancer
        Living Behind Enemy Lines Without a Map
Regina Kerschbaumer
    Yoga Coffee and a Glass of Wine
        A Yoga Journey
Gillian Perry
    Capturing the Celestial Lights
        A Practical Guide to Imagining the
        Northern Lights
Arthur Worrell
    A Grandfather's Story
        Arthur Worrell's War

# Public Affairs Books

David Bailey, John Mair and Neil Fowler (Editors)
Keeping the Wheels on the Road – Brexit Book 3
UK Auto Post Brexit

Eben Black
Lies Lobbying and Lunch
PR, Public Affairs and Political
Engagement – A Guide

Paul Davies, John Mair and Neil Fowler
Will the Tory Party Ever Be the Same? – Brexit
Book 4
The Effect of Brexit

John Mair and Neil Fowler (Editors)
Oil Dorado
Guyana's Black Gold

John Mair and Richard Keeble (Editors)
Investigative Journalism Today:
Speaking Truth to Power

John Mair and Neil Fowler (Editors)
Do They Mean Us – Brexit Book 1
The Foreign Correspondents' View of the
British Brexit

John Mair, Alex De Ruyter and Neil Fowler (Editors)
The Case for Brexit – Brexit Book 2

John Mair, Richard Keeble and Farrukh Dhondy (Editors)
V.S Naipaul:
The legacy

John Mills
Economic Growth Post Brexit
How the UK Should Take on the World

Christian Wolmar
Wolmar for London
Creating a Grassroots Campaign in a
Digital Age

# Fiction

Paul Davies
>The Ways We Live Now
>>Civil Service Corruption, Wilful Blindness, Commercial Fraud, and Personal Greed – a Novel of Our Times

Paul Davies
>Coming To
>>A Novel of Self-Realisation

Victor Hill
>Three Short Stories
>>Messages, The Gospel of Vic the Fish, The Theatre of Ghosts

# Children's Books

Chris Reeve – illustrations by Mike Tingle
>The Dictionary Boy
>>A Salutary Tale

Fredrik Payedar
>The Spirit of Chaos
>>It Begins

Manufactured by Amazon.ca
Bolton, ON